TABLE OF CONTENTS

Introduction

R aised beds can be best described as a form of garden, constructed above the natural terrain. In raised bed gardening, the soil is usually formed in 3 to 4 feet wide beds bearing any size or shape. The soil is usually enclosed within a frame, typically made of rock, wood or blocks of concrete.

These gardens improve the growing condition of the plants by elevating their roots well above the poor-quality soil. As a bonus, it takes less effort to improve the soil into being a better growing medium for the plants.

You don't have to worry about your raised beds being infiltrated by certain "obnoxious" grass or tree roots (an aspect not typically seen in your average vegetable gardens) - this because the soil used in raised bed gardening warms up faster during spring. In addition, the elevated position of raised beds prevents weed seeds from blowing into the garden soil.

In a nutshell, some of the aspects that give raised beds a distinctive advantage over other forms of gardening are:

- Less digging is required.
- Raised beds are heated better by the sun.
- Much easier weeding.
- Much easier to provide root crops such as potatoes, with the necessary room to grow.
- Better drainage means you don't have to worry about the plants being damaged due to residual water. This is why plants grown in raised bed gardens suffer less from root rot diseases.
- Because replenishing soil in raised bed gardening is comparatively much easier, you don't have to worry about nematodes and diseases. Any depleted soil can be promptly removed and replaced.
- It helps you save on resources. For example, you don't have to use fertilizer throughout the entire garden. Instead you apply them to the beds only.
- Foot traffic won't do any harm to the plants.
- Raised bed gardening is easy to learn - even if you are just

getting started.

On the flip side, the major disadvantage is the cost of building the bed walls if you want to make them durable and aesthetically pleasing. But don't worry. Later we'll discuss options for building your beds inexpensively or even free.

Choosing the right spot for your raised bed garden

Choosing the right spot for your garden will go a long way toward ensuring that it is successful. A little planning up front is well worth it. Here are the most important things to consider when choosing your garden location.

You should always opt for a sunny area to setup your raised bed garden. Typically, the longer the garden receives sunlight, the better. Any site that receives 6-7 hours of sunlight should be avoided. Anything above that and your crops will be much happier.

Any nearby trees will also be competing against your raised beds for sunlight. It is recommended that you choose a site away from drip lines of trees (this is the furthest reach of its leaves). Also, consider how the sun moves throughout the day to avoid putting your garden right in the shade of the tree. In the northern hemisphere, placing your garden to the south of your trees and out from under the drip line, will ensure that the tree does not block any sun from your plants.

These same guidelines apply to houses, fences, hillsides, or any other structure that will block needed sunlight from shining on your plants.

If you can't find a suitable sunny place for your raised beds, you should stick to growing cool season vegetables such as cabbages, broccoli, and lettuce. This is because cool season vegetables are better suited to growing in shade.

In addition, your site of choice should provide wind protection to the plants. This is particularly important because springtime winds can be disastrous for the tender stems of your young plants. Similarly, strong summer winds may dry out plants excessively. Some air circulation is good, just protect against heavy winds.

Therefore, always make it a point to have a border of shrubs or a fence in order to reduce the wind speed. You can also create your own artificial windbreak from easily available high-density polyethylene plastic mesh. This is the same type of plastic used to barricade the area around a construction site. A well designed windbreak usually lowers plant stress, which in turn results in quicker and better yields.

The beds should not be located in frost pockets or places with no air circulation because that may inevitably make your plants vulnerable to fungal diseases. Also, avoid places where fire ants or other infestations are a problem because you certainly won't like the outcome if they chose to build nests in your bed-soil.

Finally, be sure to locate the garden near a quality water source. This one seems obvious, but is an essential requirement for successful raised bed gardening. Despite having a number of distinct advantages over traditional vegetable gardening, the plants in a raised bed garden tends to dry out way quicker due to their higher elevation and improved drainage.

Bottom-line

1. Choose a sunny place so plants can get at least 6-7 hours sunlight, or more, every day.
2. If the site of your choice doesn't have any natural protection against wind, build one.
3. Try avoiding any location near drip lines of trees.
4. Places in frost pockets or with low air circulation should be avoided.
5. Consider the convenience of your water source when locating your raised bed garden.

Tools and Materials

Before you start making those garden beds, it's best for you to know which tools and materials you will need. This way, you'll know exactly what you should buy—and understand the purpose of each.

Lumber

For each side of the bed, you will need to get some cedar boards. You can use 2 x 6. 2 x 8, or 2 x 4. However, you should keep in mind that 2 x 6 is often recommended because it is sturdy enough to handle the buildup of soil.

Next, you can use 4 x 4-inch cedar wood, cut 10" longer than the size of the bed that you have in mind. Remember that the longer the bed, the more posts you need. You can also ask people at the Lumber Yard to cut them for you if you're not too sure about about cutting them yourself.

Cross Supports

For these, you'll need ½" of aluminum flat stock. You need two screws for the mid-span posts, and 6 for each corner. Use a drill and hardware screws for this.

Fastenings

You'll need coated deck screws that are 3.5" in size for this one. For each corner, you need two midspan posts, and 6 screws for both of those corners. 1" stainless screws are recommended for these.

Other Tools

Other tools that you need include drill, hacksaw, screwdriver, sledge/mallet, carpenter's level, square, and hand saw.

Questions before Starting

How long should the bed be?

The length of the beds will always depend on you, but you can keep in mind that the recommended standard size shouldn't go wider than 4' across, so that you won't have a hard time planting. Extremely long beds will make it hard for you to reach the farthest corners—so just stick to the standard size instead.

Make sure that cross supports are installed for every 4 to 6' length of the bed so that bowing would be prevented. However, you can try making longer beds if you know that you have a lot of space in your garden—so you can maximize the said space.

How tall should it be?

As for the height, experts say you can make it as tall as 36" but most people are fine with just 11", because it's perfect for those boards with 2 x 6" sizes. Take note, though, that sometimes, roots go so deep down the soil so it might be good to cut down on height. Some people have also said that 6" tall beds have worked for them, so you might want to try that out, too.

You may also consult a chart for soil depth, which will help you know how deep the soil should be for certain types of vegetables and other plants. There are three categories for this, which are 12 to 18" or Shallow Rooting, 18 to

24" or Medium Rooting, and 24 to 36" and up, or Deep Rooting.

For Shallow Rooting, you have strawberries, spinach, radishes, potatoes, chives, leeks, onions, lettuce, bok choy, kohlrabi, garlic, endive, corn, Chinese cabbage, celery, cauliflower, cabbage, broccoli, and arugula.

For Medium Rooting, you have turnips, squash, summer squash, peppers, peas, kale, eggplant, cucumber, chard, carrots, cantaloupe, beets, snap beans, snap peas, pole beans, and dry beans.

And for Deep Rooting, you have watermelon, tomatoes, sweet potatoes, winter squash, rhubarb, pumpkins, parsnips, okra, lima beans, asparagus, and artichokes.

Take note that even if they're in beds already, you should still make it a point to arrange those beds in such a way that larger plants won't block smaller plants from getting sunlight. For example, lettuce should be on the southernmost part of the garden, followed by medium-sized plants, and tall/climbing plants in the back row, such as pole beans and tomatoes.

What about the wood? Is Cedar the only one that can be used?

Cedar is the recommended type because it stays strong for a long time, without blocking sunlight or water from letting the plants grow. Cedar is also rot-resistant, which makes it perfect for gardening.

The best types of Cedar Wood that you can use include Juniper, Port Yellow, Vermont White, and Western Red Cedar. Red Cedar can actually last up to 15 years!

If Cedar is not available, you can also go for Redwood. However, it would be likely that Cedar is more readily available than Redwood is because sources for Redwood are usually limited.

Tips for pests and disease control

There are numerous known pests and diseases that are capable of affecting your raised bed, so you have to be alert at every point in time. Ensuring that your plants are as strong and healthy is one measure to combat the influx of pest and diseases into the garden. You also have to be alert to any possible signs that may show that pests have begun an invasion in your garden and also act appropriately.

In this chapter we will go through some of the most prevalent threats that you should be on the lookout for and measures to be taken to prevent them from spreading.

Chapter 1
Planning your Garden

What to Consider?

- Location
- Size
- Height
- Drainage

Don't think because you have limited space you can't build a raised bed. Having the luxury of space in your plot will obviously give you more options as far as planning goes but you can reap a high yield from a property with a small space so there is no need to think it won't work for you.

Even with a patio you can create raised garden beds that will not only be productive in their yield but also give beautiful definition to the area. You will have to make certain design decisions and planning is an integral part of your raised bed gardening success with this design but don't be daunted, as what you are creating is the optimum environment for your crops to grow in.

In essence that is your overall goal for having a raised bed, as a raised bed will increase your crop yield while reducing the work you need to do to get there. The location and planning at the beginning of the process will pay dividends at the end but is integral as the first step in getting there as even with bad, or no soil you can create an edible garden to be proud of.

Space permitting, you want your raised bed to be roughly three to four feet wide and seven to eight feet long. This will give you room to reach over the raised bed from the sides to tend your crops as you don't want to kneel or stand on any part of your growing area.

With a raised bed system getting the right height is also of vital importance, by creating a raised bed you are eliminating many of the usual complaints gardeners have, bending, kneeling and accidentally walking or stepping on the garden beds!

Getting the soil into the optimum condition is something I remember my grandparents facing on a monthly and yearly basis. Traditionally if you are faced with compacted or clay soil, for example, you could spend hours digging in and trying to perfect the soil to plant your vegetables, and seasonally you will have to continue this process! So, by building a raised bed system, you are eliminating this hurdle right away as you can build your raised bed right on top of that troublesome soil and then make your own soil - location permitting.

Many gardeners have found that growing crops in raised beds rather than traditional ground beds can yield twice the harvest. The main reason for this is that plants respond better in looser, rich soil giving room for the roots to grow easily and along with the fertile soil, the raised bed gives good drainage.

Having a raised bed also stops soil compaction to maintain soil aeration at its optimum that traditional ground beds tend to suffer from.

As planting crops in traditional ground beds will inevitably lead to the soil getting compacted just by you walking along and planting/weeding each month or season, affecting the soil structure.

This is why the size and height are so important when planning your raised bed as you want to be able to reach over easily to plant your crops without any contact with the soil, also the fact you are building the raised bed with nutrient-rich soil and using compost just for your crops to grow in is of huge benefit to their quality, and this is a soil mix you will create instead of trying to perfect or alter your existing soil.

When thinking about the location of your raised bed, it's worth noting you need six to eight hours of sunlight for optimum growing conditions, so have a look at potential areas taking particular notice of any walls, fences or tree canopy's that may inhibit your raised bed from getting sunlight. Of course, this will change season to season but planning for sufficient sunlight is your aim here as too little and you will have stunted growth, or worse, no growth.

While planning my raised bed area I found this simple exercise of huge benefit, as it saved lots of work and heartache over time.

Draw a rough plan of your garden and note where the sun hits over a day at say 8 am, 10 am, 12 pm, 2 pm, and 4 pm. This will give you a good idea of the area or areas to build your raised bed based upon a full six to eight hours of sunlight per day if you find you have reduced sunlight or you are in a part of the world where seasons affect sunlight exposure throughout the year, then this is even more imperative you get this right.

Don't be scared if you don't have the full 8 hours of sunlight per day, but try to aim for the maximum within your garden perimeter, but unfortunately, this may mean you need to reign in your enthusiasm and undertake research for a couple of days instead, the beauty of this is that if you discover you only get 2-4 hours of sunlight per day in the area you want to grow your crops you may have to change strategy however if that is all you have to work with i.e. built-up areas, high garden walls, etc., don't worry as there is still an awful amount of food or flowers you can grow.

Once you have selected the perfect area in your garden, grab a blank piece of paper, and with a pencil, draw your house and garden on it. With a compass (or smartphone app) find North and South, which are important, as you want your garden south facing to provide maximum sun exposure. Dependent on how much lawn (if you have one) you want to keep, highlight this as a no-grow zone and then what's left allocate for your garden beds. This may be a little bit of a dynamic situation as it's still going to depend on how much sun get's to these areas so please take your time, once this is done, just circle the areas and you have got the start of your raised bed system.

Another design feature to think about is drainage of your raised bed as it is also an important factor to the success of the yield, the simple fact of raising the bed will aid the drainage, preventing waterlogging and maintaining the nutrient-rich soil you have added, think of your raised bed as a huge plant pot that without drainage will create an anaerobic environment, this will be further accelerated in heavy rains, making it hard for your plants roots to breathe, this will mean that the roots can't get the oxygen they need and so start to rot and therefore won't grow and thrive, as you want them to.

So again, getting the size and height of your raised bed is essential, once you have decided on the size and location of your raised bed, you must consider the height as this will help you with determining the optimal drainage as most vegetables don't have long root systems; therefore don't need deep beds. Generally speaking, the worse condition of the underlying soil, the deeper you will want the raised bed. The deeper the bed, the greater the volume of soil mix needed and therefore, more moisture, which in theory will reduce watering needs.

Determining the Height of the Raised Bed

It's worth noting that the height or depth of your raised bed will, in turn, dictate what you can or can't grow. A shallow height will mean the root structure of your plants may be inhibited due to the fact they will reach a barrier if the underlying ground is impacted. You may need to consider a barrier if you don't want your plant's roots to grow in the compacted or inferior soil and not in your nutrient-rich soil mix you have created for your raised bed.

Examples of Depths per Plant Type

- 6-10 Inches
- Basil
- Beet
- Carrot short
- Chervil
- Chives
- Cilantro
- Lettuce
- Onion
- Greens
- Parsley

- Radish
- Peppermint
- Spinach
- Thyme
- Dwarf cherry tomato
- Watercress
- Oregano
- Sage
- Majoram
- 10-15 Inches
- Carrot
- Celery
- Cabbage
- Garlic
- Chard
- Leek
- Lettuce
- Mustard
- Oregano
- Potato
- Strawberry
- Dwarf patio tomato
- 15-18 Inches
- Beans
- Collards
- Cucumber
- Kale
- Pea
- Pepper
- Squash

- Short Vine tomato
- 18-24 Inches
- Broccoli
- Brussel sprouts
- Cabbage
- Corn
- Cauliflower
- Tomato

As an example, raised bed heights can be as little as 6 inches and as much as 36 inches, it is up to you at what height to work at to save your back and make life easier but if you work on the fact you need roughly 16 inches or 40 cm's of rich topsoil for your plants root systems to grow you won't go far wrong.

The next step is to ensure you have added a drainage system below this topsoil, I prefer using organic matter to act as the drainage such as foliage, logs, etc. but you can use aggregates such as crushed granite, sand or small pebbles and rock, or a combination of the two.

The benefit of using organic matter as a base layer drainage system is that you can source most if not all of it for free. If you don't have any on your property, ask your neighbors or ring up a local tree company for offcuts that are no good for mulch or firewood. Most are happy to give them to you if you can pick them up. Also the more organic matter you use in a deeper bed (roughly 60 cm/ 24 inches /2 feet) the less rich topsoil you need to add, this will save you a lot on your costs especially if you have more than one bed to build, but more on this a little later.

Now you have the size, height, location, and drainage planned another consideration is getting the base of your raised bed right. If your garden has a base, in other words, it's not open to the ground, for example directly onto concrete or patios, irrespective of how deep it is you will need some type of drainage. Otherwise, it becomes one big wet mess, which will rot your plants. Normally drainage holes are situated at the base to allow water to drain away, however as they block up occasionally routine maintenance is required. Just to clarify as I said earlier about using fill to bulk up the base of your bed to save on topsoil.

Just be aware if you are in temporary accommodation or renting, or if you will possibly move the bed, the more logs, landfill, etc. that you use makes it a bit of a pain when you have to take them down and move them, so think hard before you plan.

Chapter 2
Structure and construction

Building a Raised Bed Garden

A raised bed can be built with any one of a number of materials, the most popular being timber (treated or untreated). Other materials include, concrete, brick, corrugated sheet metal, sandbags, straw bales or concrete block work. In fact anything that you have to hand that can produce a decent barrier between 4 inched (100mm) and 2 foot (600mm) inches high, can be used to construct a Raised Bed garden.

Raised Bed Dimensions:

As to dimensions, this is really determined by many things including the space you have available, and indeed just exactly what your requirements are. Do you have a large family to feed, or do you intend to sell or barter (bartering is a great way to enjoy a diversity of produce from other gardeners) some of your produce?

With all that considered, a typical raised bed vegetable plot is about 6 foot by 3 foot. This is an ideal size because it allows access from both sides, without you having to step onto the raised bed itself. This enables you to tend to your plants without treading on them in the process – always a good thing!

Another popular size is a simple square arrangement around 4 foot (1200mm) square to produce what has become known as a square foot garden. This simple technique can produce an amazing variety of vegetables throughout the growing season

As to depth. Overall you should aim for a minimum of4 inches for a simple herb garden say, and up to 2 foot for root vegetables such as carrots and parsnips.

Bear in mind that the depth of the raised bed does not have to be the height of the sides, to explain a bit further. Say you would like a bed depth of 18 inches (450mm), but you only have timber for 12 inch sides.

It should perhaps be pointed out here though, that this negates the concept of building a raised bed for the advantages to be gained with the height of the bed itself above ground, as will be explained later in the article. This system is mainly used where the existing soil is of poor quality and has to be replaced/substituted in order to grow the vegetables of your choice.

If you are building multiple raised beds, then they should be placed at least two feet (600mm) apart if possible – more if wheelchair access is required - to allow for easy access between them.

RAISED BED BEING BUILT WITH DECKING MATERIAL

Building a Timber Raised Bed

The construction of a timber raised bed is fairly simple and straight forward. First of all, level and mark out the area where you would like your raised bed to be. Bear in mind that it should not be under overhanging trees, and in an area where you can have easy access for tending your plants. It should get a minimum of 5-6 hours sunshine per day to produce best results for most vegetables.

For a 6 x 3 x 1.5 foot bed built using traditional decking timber, (I tend to use decking as it is stronger than just plain boards) you will need:

- 6 lengths decking @ 6' x 6" x 1"

* 6 lengths decking @ 2'10" x 6" x 1"
* 10 – 3" x 2" pointed posts @ 30"
* Weed control fabric
* Galvanized screws or nails
* Wire mesh (optional)

Although the following instructions are aimed at an 'anchored' bed, it is also acceptable to simply make the corner posts the same depth as the bed itself, and lay the whole frame on the ground – the weight of soil will usually keep it anchored in place.

Begin by marking out with string and pegs, the area of your raised bed, putting down a peg on each corner. This is where you should consider whether or not you are going to dig out any of the existing ground.

Questions to ask yourself are, what depth of compost do I need, versus what height do I want the finished bed to be. If you are growing root vegetables that need depth, but you do not want the finished height to be over 1 foot for instance, then digging out the area to the depth required is your only option. This 'digging out' however may not be necessary if you have good quality topsoil. Simply loosen the existing soil with a garden fork and add your infill mix (more on this later) to the required level.

Once this decision is made, then we can proceed with building the raised bed. Once you have the pegs in the area that marks out the four corners of your raised bed, you simply take out one peg at a time and replace by hammering down your pointed posts, leaving them a minimum of 18 inches above the ground.

Alternatively, if you make these posts longer then you can use them as handy aids for lifting yourself up when tending your vegetables – just a matter of choice really.

The best way to do this is to put down one post at the end, then temporarily fix the first short end against the post. With this done, then hammer in the second post flush with the end of the 6" x 2" decking plank. Proceed with the two longer sides, then complete the other end. If you just put one screw partially home, then you can easily adjust to suit.

Be sure that you have leveled the timber and that you have left a minimum 12" in height above the first planks, so you are able to complete the job.

I find that it is better to construct with a cordless screwdriver as this does not impact the framework in the same way that hammer and nails does. Also should you make a slight error, then it is no trouble to take apart for adjustment.

Once this is done then simply mark out along the inside length two feet from each end, then making sure the construction is straight, hammer in two of the posts to the same height as the others. On the end of the construction, do the same with one post in the centre of the framework.

This will give you a strong sturdy construction, which you will need if you do not want the sides of your raised deck to bow under the pressure of the soil.

Point of note:

If you are building with heavier timbers, say 6" x 2" for instance then it may be possible to just put one post in the center of the long side and none at all on the end. I however tend to lean on the cautious side, and would rather aim for stronger option overall. Another tip is to put a cross brace in, if you are concerned about the sides bowing outward.

It is not an exact science, but there are minimum guidelines that must be kept to ensure a construction fit for purpose.

After you have built the sides then just screw down the remaining planking face down along the edge (as in the photograph), to make a comfortable sitting or leaning area for tending to your raised bed.

One thing to consider during this time, is whether or not you are bothered by Gophers or Moles. If you are, then at this point you would place in 1" galvanized wire mesh, covering the bottom of your raised bed. This will be extremely effective in stopping the varmints from destroying your crop and giving you endless grief and heartache!

The weed control fabric should be fixed down the inside of the bed, to keep the wet soil away from the timber. This will help the timber to breathe and make it just that bit longer lasting.

2nd Point of note: Do not use timber that has been treated with creosote, as this may weep through and kill the plants!

If you think you may wish to move them to another location perhaps in the next season, then it is probably best not to hammer the corner posts into the ground and instead make them the actual height of the bed itself.

In other words your 18 inch high bed will just need 18 inch high posts instead of 30 inches or so. These will be fixed in the same way to the corner posts and the infill will hold the whole construction in place – though not as well as the former method!

Here is an example of a larger construction 9 foot in length and 18 inches high. As you can see, this bed is built to sit upon a concrete base. Built with three rows of decking, it has 2 centre braces made from 3 x 2 to keep it solid.

Possibly the simplest form of Raised Bed is the 4 foot square model. This can be constructed from decking material by simply adding a short corner post at each corner and fixing it together with decking screws. Everything else is constructed the same way as the larger deck.

- Materials needed would be:
- 2 lengths decking @ 4' x 6" x 1"
- 2 lengths decking @ 3'10" x 6" x 1"
- 4 – 2" x 2" pointed posts @ 18"
- Weed control fabric
- Galvanized screws or nails

- Wire mesh (optional)

Again, you have the option to simply use 6 inch posts at the corners if you have no need to 'lock in' to the ground area.

To create a 'Square Foot Garden then simply add a 'grid' as in the picture below using garden canes or even twine to mark out the foot-square areas for planting.

Regarding Timber: Some people have concerns over whether or not to use treated or untreated timber to build their Raised Beds. This is perfectly understandable as more of us become aware of the possibility of contamination regarding chemicals that have been used to treat the timbers.

There are 2 main issues to consider here, and that is the effect that treated timber may have on the plants themselves. And the effect that may be had to the consumer of these same vegetables – if indeed they survive!

Modern timber treatment via tantalization methods according to the soil association (www.soilassociation.org) is perfectly suitable for gardening structures such as Raised Beds or compost bins – provided the timber has been purchased already treated.

Chapter 3
The Terrain

Raised Bed Gardens: Soil Preparation

Every successful gardener will tell you that soil preparation comes first when you aim for a bountiful harvest. Without proper soil, you may as well throw in the towel before you even begin. Initially you should focus all your attention on the condition and quality of soil you are going to use. A good quality soil will ensure that your vegetable plants grow to their full potential and that you will not spend too much valuable time fighting pests and weeds.

Following are a few tips for mixing rich and fertile soil to suit all your planters and garden beds. Your locality may influence the type of soil you will need to a small degree, but these basic principles are applicable everywhere, regardless of where you live.

1.Topsoil does not Always Contain Organic Matter

Purchased soil often looks quite promising: dark in color, well screened and clean. This might not always be an indication of what it actually contains. It may well be a good growing medium though without any of the vital organic matter that is essential for growth. Therefore, you should always inquire from the attendant at the garden center what the soil consists of and what its origin is. You should assume that some extra feeding would be necessary to build up this soil to the standards needed for successful gardening.

2. Revitalize Soil Annually

Usually new gardens will do fairly well during their initial year even though no additional matter was added to amend the soil. The reason for this is that the available nutrients, organic matter and trace minerals have not been tapped yet. However, after one or two seasons of successive gardening, the crops will have used up all the riches in the soil. That is why it is so important that you revitalize your gardening soil regularly.

A wonderful solution is to plant 'green manure' as a cover crop after the first two seasons of growing vegetables. These crops are very easy and simple to grow and have many benefits. As soon as the cover crop has matured, chop it up and then dig it lightly into your soil. Now your soil has been replenished with fresh organic matter. Consider growing leguminous crops like alfalfa or fenugreek since they will fix the atmospheric nitrogen in such a way that it can be used as nutrients by the plants. This type of green manure has many benefits; their roots will loosen the soil, bringing the deeper nutrients nearer to the surface of your garden beds. While you chop up the manure and work it into the ground as well as the activity of the roots will aerate your soil, thus improving the drainage for future crops.

3.Soil must be Crumbly, Fluffy and Light

You want to make it as easy as possible for the roots of your plants to be able to work their way through the layers of soil in search of moisture and nutrients. Compacted and dense soil will make this essential task of plant roots very difficult and they will spend so much energy struggling to get to the nutrients that not much will be left for the rest of the plant to grow. You can easily facilitate better root growth by lightening your garden soil. This is turn will lead to better vegetative growth and you will see the positive results when your plants start to flourish.

How do you know if your soil is light enough? A simple test is to push your finger into it. You should have no trouble to poke it in up to the third knuckle of the finger. If you struggle to achieve this then you will have to lighten the soil by adding peat moss and working it into the top layer. I have already mentioned that peat moss is acidic by nature, so you will most probably have to add lime. Always enquire about the pH level of the soil you purchase. You need to know if lime will be necessary. Acidic soil is commonly found in most areas of our country so lime is usually needed, although there are regions that have alkaline soil. Many gardeners prefer to use vermiculite for lightening the soil because it does not break down at the same speedy rate as the peat moss.

4.The Ultimate Amendment for Soil: Compost

Making your own compost is easy and can save you extra expense. Many gardeners have a compost heap in their back gardens. Compost consists of organic material filled with nutrients to turn normal soil into a rich medium for all your plants.Use this valuable resource correctly and wisely and you can be sure of a prolific vegetable garden. Instead of adding compost to the soil right after harvesting, rather postpone it to two or three weeks before you plant your next crop. You want to prevent a sudden downpour from washing away all that wonderful richness in the compost and undo all your hard work.

The general idea amongst many people who consider a compost heap an unsightly, smelly mess is truly a misconception. If you go about it the correct way, your compost heap will be neat and tidy with a wonderful rich and earthy aroma. Veteran gardeners will tell you that active compost heaps should not be smelly. If your plot is too small to allow for a larger compost pile, you can purchase a sealed composter. This device contains smells and is small and tidy in appearance. Because they are sealed, they are immune to dogs, mice, raccoons and such-like critters.

A composter in your garden has an additional benefit; it will take care of all the dead plant matter left after the harvest. After your last tomatoes have been harvested, carefully remove all the 'skeletons' from the plants, break or chop it into smaller pieces and simply throw them into the compost pile. It is a wonderful way to re-use all plant residues in your garden to make a contribution to the nutrient-rich compost for your future crops. Just inspect the dead plant matter carefully for any diseases before you add it to the composter.

5.Organic Fertilizers are the Best Choice

Do not be overly enticed by all the many product claims you read on the packaging of chemical fertilizers. They may be true, but the advantages often do not last and are rather short-lived. You will have to reapply them regularly after each planting. In the end, the benefits of these commercial fertilizers may be lessened to some extend because they do not improve the condition of the soil, the most important aspect of successful gardening.

I would therefore suggest that when you find yourself short of compost, to make use of an organic fertilizer. It will also give your little seedlings an instant boost. Canola meal is one of the popular fertilizers. This material is finely ground and lightweight, making it very easy to sprinkle onto your beds. On top of that, it is relatively inexpensive and free of weeds. (Some kinds of manures may include weeds). Make sure to mix the canola meal lightly into the topsoil because mice love it and may attack your beds. For the same reason, take care where you store your bag. It should be well sealed and in any dry spot where mice will not be able to reach.

6.Rock Phosphate

If you a new gardener, using the plot or raised bed for the first time, you will probably be able to use the basic soil for one or two years. After this, you will have to add some source of phosphorus to it. Your crops will grow steadily and vigorously and mature early because of the addition of this element. You will have larger-sized vegetables and fruit in autumn. Crops, which mature earlier, will better avoid summer drought and be less vulnerable to disease and frost. Rock phosphate also contains a number of minor elements like zinc, boron, iodine and nickel, all necessary in smaller doses for plants to grow optimally. Furthermore, rock phosphate works long-term, thus releases its elements slowly so that the plant will benefit over a longer period.

Although phosphate is such an essential contributor to plant growth it is often overlooked even by more experienced gardeners. I strongly advise you to buy a bag and sprinkle a handful or two into your beds from time to time. A sack of phosphate will store well and last for years. Make a note to mix some rock phosphate into your raised vegetable beds at least every couple of years.

After reading this chapter, I am sure you understand the importance of paying attention to all the different aspects of your soil; its structure, the organic matter it contains, its drainage and the condition of the bottom or ground soil. If you focus on these elements all your expectations for a lush, high-yielding vegetable garden will be met. Your time will be spent on harvesting rather than on fighting diseases and pests and you will end up a happy, contented gardener.

Chapter 4
Types of Plants

Root Vegetables

Root vegetables such as carrots, beets, parsnips, radishes and so on do well in raised beds. Carrots and parsnips grow deep roots, so you either need an eight to twelve inch deep raised bed or you need to have dug down into the soil below to give them the space they need to grow. The deeper root vegetables will not work if you have a shallow bed and either poor soil beneath it or a wire mesh to prevent burrowing pests. Raise your beds up higher (12" is fine) to grow deep rooted veg if the soil below is poor. Because raised beds tend to be free of rocks, you end up with good quality carrots and parsnips with long, well-formed roots. Add horticultural sand to your raised beds to make it drain better, so your carrots grow straighter.

Leafy Greens

Most leafy greens such as kale, spinach, cauliflower, lettuce and so on do fantastically in a raised bed. Many of these can be started early in the year, and some, such as kale, pak choi, cauliflower, broccoli, and others can be started later in the year and overwintered. Because raised beds warm faster than the surrounding soil you can often get a good harvest before summer and they will do very well because they like free draining soil.

Onions, Leeks, and Garlic

Any member of the onion family does well in a raised bed because they like plenty of organic matter and a free draining soil. They do tend to have a long growing season (grown from seed they can take over 100 days to mature) and raised beds ensure that you can get planting early in the year.

The onion family does not like competition nor do they like drying out. Make sure you keep the weeds down because they will crowd out the onions. In hot weather, water these beds regularly because if they dry out too much, the plants will end up dying and the bulbs will not form properly.

Tomatoes

Tomatoes are greedy feeders and, if you add extra compost to your raised bed, then they will do very well indeed. However, the only issue comes with staking the tomatoes as the stakes are not secure in the loose soil. You can either drive the stakes into the firm soil below your raised bed or fix them to the edges of the bed. I have screwed wooden trellises to the raised bed as support for plants, which worked very well.

Peas and Beans

These will do very well in raised beds though you may have issues with supporting taller crops such as runner beans. Driving supports into the soil beneath your bed or fixing them to the bed itself will help.

Young plants are at risk of damage from birds so will need covering and protecting. With beans you will need to build a frame from bamboo canes, using ten to twelve foot high canes for them to climb up. Either lash short canes to these or build a frame of garden twine to help encourage the beans to spread and climb up.

Vine Crops

These are not very well suited for raised beds, particularly as squashes are very greedy feeders indeed. The problem with long trailing vines is you run out of space, and they can crowd out neighboring plants. You can build supports for them, and you can grow your cucumbers vertically (see later in the book) which will help reduce the space requirements.

Courgettes (zucchini) are available in bush forms which do not take up as much space as the trailing forms and are well suited for raised beds. Other squash plants, such as petty pan squashes, are reasonably compact plants which makes them suitable for a raised bed.

Herbs

Herbs grow very well in raised beds, and you can make a fantastic herb garden in them. Herbs such as marjoram, lavender, and rosemary are excellent at attracting pollinating insects, making them an ideal addition to your vegetable plot.

Herbs do not need to take part in any crop rotation scheme. Although many herbs are annuals and will need re-sowing every year, others are perennial and can stay in place permanently with some pruning at the end of each growing season.

Bay trees, lavender, marjoram, rosemary, thyme and many others will last for many years. Remember that bay trees are just that ... trees, and so they grow very tall unless they are pruned and kept under control. Rosemary and lavender both benefit from a good prune at the end of the growing season otherwise they become woody and leggy with fewer flowers.

Growing Flowers in Raised Beds

Raised beds are ideal for growing flowers in. Many people like to grow flowers either instead of or as well as vegetables.

As with most other plants, different flowers prefer different soil types and conditions. By grouping together flowers with similar requirements in the same bed, you can ensure that they all thrive and produce beautiful blooms.

It is important to remember that your flowers will grow and fill your raised bed. You must leave enough space between each plant initially so that they can grow without crowding out your other flowers. As with your herb bed, your flower beds will look bare to start with but avoid the temptation to fill the space, the plants will expand, and your raised bed will be awash with color.

How To Grow Some Of The Plants

ASPARAGUS

Asparagus does not like to compete with weeds, so maintain your bed well. Asparagus plants can live 15 or more years, producing every year once they are established.

- **Growing Seasons:** early spring, plant 4 to 6 weeks before last frost
- **Spacing:** 12 to 18 inches apart
- **Seed to Harvest:** plant seedlings (crowns) the first year; harvest lightly in the second spring
- **Earliest Outdoor planting:** early spring once your raised bed can be worked
- **Watering:** water regularly

Try growing the large-leaf basil for making wraps and purple basil for creating a focal spot in your garden.

- **Growing Seasons:** spring, late spring

- **Spacing:** 12 to 18 inches

- **Seed to Harvest:** 50 to 90 days

- **Earliest Outdoor Planting:** after danger of frost; ground should be 60 degrees Fahrenheit

- **Watering:** needs 1 inch of water per week during the growth cycle

Beet greens and roots are edible. They can be roasted, pickled, grilled, or boiled, and they freeze well.

- **Growing Seasons:** early spring or late fall in warmer climates; late spring or early fall in colder climates

- **Spacing:** 12 inches apart

- **Seed to Harvest:** 50 to 60 days

- **Earliest Outdoor Planting:** in cooler climates, early spring once your raised bed can be worked; in frost-free areas, sow in the fall

- **Watering:** 1 inch of water per week

<u>BROCCOLI</u>

If you live in a warm climate, a fall planting is best, because broccoli thrives in cool weather.

- **Growing Seasons:** spring, fall, cool weather

- **Spacing:** 18 to 24 inches in rows 3 feet apart

- **Seed to Harvest:** 45 to 60 days

- **Earliest Outdoor Planting:** 2 weeks before the last spring frost;

in fall, in warm climates, 85 to 100 days before the first frost

- **Watering:** moderate and even; water only the roots, not the heads

CABBAGE

Some varieties of cabbage grow flowers. The leaves of those plants are edible, but they are usually used as a garnish. Check your seed packets to verify you have edible cabbage leaves.

- **Growing Seasons:** plant in early spring, late fall
- **Spacing:** 12 to 18 inches apart

- **Seed to Harvest:** 50 to 60 days

- **Earliest Outdoor Planting:** early spring once your raised bed can be worked

- **Watering:** keep well-watered during dry periods

<u>CARROT</u>

Plant carrots every couple of weeks for nonstop harvesting.

- **Growing Seasons:** spring, fall, depending on location; check your zone for specific times

- **Spacing:** 3 to 4 inches apart in rows 1 to 2 feet apart

- **Seed to Harvest:** 50 to 80 days

- **Earliest Outdoor Planting:** after danger of heavy frost; in frost-free areas plant in fall

- **Watering:** keep moist but not saturated; best done by drip irrigation; do not water foliage

CHIVES

Chives are a great focal point in a garden bed and a welcome addition to many cuisines. For best production and healthiest plants, divide clumps every

3 to 4 years.

- **Growing Seasons:** spring, late spring

- **Spacing:** 3 to 4 inches apart

- **Seed to Harvest:** 80 to 90 days

- **Earliest Outdoor Planting:** after danger of heavy frost

- **Watering:** water seedlings thoroughly after planting; plants need about 1 inch of water per week

CILANTRO

Cilantro can be harvested as cilantro (the fresh herb) or coriander (the seed).

For cilantro, harvest plants once green leaves are present, before the plants flower. For coriander, harvest the seeds once they turn grayish-brown.

- **Growing Seasons:** spring, early summer
- **Spacing:** 10 to 14 inches
- **Seed to Harvest:** 60 to 90 days
- **Earliest Outdoor Planting:** after danger of frost
- **Watering:** needs 1 inch of water per week

CORN

Keep different varieties away from one another so they do not cross-pollinate, which could affect the flavor and quality of your harvested corn.

- **Growing Seasons:** spring, late spring
- **Spacing:** 5 to 6 inches in rows 2 to 3 feet apart
- **Seed to Harvest:** 70 to 85 days
- **Earliest Outdoor Planting:** after danger of frost
- **Watering:** needs 1 to 2 inches of water per week during the growth cycle; soaker hose or drip irrigation is best

CUCUMBER

Cucumber plants are prolific, so do not plant too many. Buy pickling cucumber seeds to make pickles and slicing cucumber seeds to eat fresh. Do not use slicing cucumbers to make pickles; they soften when pickled.

- **Growing Seasons:** soil temperature at least 60 degrees Fahrenheit

- **Spacing:** 18 to 36 inches apart; bush varieties can be planted closer together

- **Seed to Harvest:** 50 to 70 days

- **Earliest Outdoor Planting:** after the last frost

- **Watering:** steady supply of water; drip irrigation on a timer is best

GREEN BEANS

Beans are available as bush beans or pole beans. Bush beans do not need the support of a trellis, but pole beans do.

- **Growing Seasons:** early to late spring, depending on zone; check your zone for specific times

- **Spacing:** 2 to 4 inches apart

- **Seed to Harvest:** 50 to 55 days

- **Earliest Outdoor Planting:** early spring once the danger of frost has passed

- **Watering:** 1 inch per week

KALE

Kale has many health benefits. It is good for digestion, high in iron and vitamin K, and filled with antioxidants. You can plant it from early spring to early summer, but if you plant it in late summer, you can harvest it from fall until the first ground freeze.

- **Growing Seasons:** spring, fall
- **Spacing:** 12 to 18 inches apart
- **Seed to Harvest:** 50 to 55 days

- **Earliest Outdoor Planting:** early spring once your raised bed can be worked; will germinate as low as 45 degrees Fahrenheit

- **Watering:** do not let the plants dry out during drought periods

LEEK

Leeks grow through the winter in the Deep South. Some varieties are bred to overwinter in colder eastern climates.

- **Growing Seasons:** spring, fall

- **Spacing:** 18 to 20 inches apart

- **Seed to Harvest:** 98 to 105 days

- **Earliest Outdoor Planting:** 4 weeks before last frost

- **Watering:** 1 inch of water per week; keep evenly watered

LETTUCE

Lactuca sativa

Lettuce comes in leaf or head varieties, and each type offers diverse colors, shapes of leaves, and flavors to choose from.

- **Growing Seasons:** fall, summer, depending on zone; check your zone for specific times

- **Spacing:** 6 to 12 inches

- **Seed to Harvest:** 45 to 75 days

- **Earliest Outdoor Planting:** after danger of frost

- **Watering:** water deeply at least once a week

ONION

Onions can be harvested as green onions or, if grown to full maturity, as bulbs.

- **Growing Seasons:** spring, fall, depending on location; check your zone for specific times

- **Spacing:** 3 to 4 inches apart in rows 1 to 2 feet apart

- **Seed to Harvest:** when planting seeds, 100 to 150 days; when planting seeds for green onions, 60 to 120 days; when planting onion sets (young plants), harvest at desired size as green onions or in 85 to 100 days as bulbs

- **Earliest Outdoor Planting:** after danger of heavy frost

- **Watering:** keep the roots wet and tops dry; watering by ditch or drip irrigation is best

PARSNIP

For the sweetest flavor, plant parsnips after a light frost.

- **Growing Seasons:** spring or fall in frost-free zones

- **Spacing:** 12 inches apart

- **Seed to Harvest:** 105 days

- **Earliest Outdoor Planting:** early spring once your raised bed can be worked

- **Watering:** 1 inch of water per week

PEAS

Snow peas should be picked before the pod is full of enlarged peas. Shelling peas should be picked after the peas start to enlarge, but before they are ready to break open the pod.

- **Growing Seasons:** in warmer climates, late winter; in cooler climates, early spring

- **Spacing:** 1 to 4 inches apart in rows 18 inches apart
- **Seed to Harvest:** 68 to 75 days
- **Earliest Outdoor Planting:** early spring once your raised bed can be worked
- **Watering:** soil should be moist; heavy watering when the peas are flowering can decrease production

POTATO

Purchase seed potatoes from a nursery. Do not use potatoes from the grocery; they have been treated to prevent sprouting.

- **Growing Seasons:** spring, fall

- **Spacing:** plant in a trench 6 to 8 inches deep; place seed potatoes at 12 to 18 inches; allow 2 to 3 feet between rows

- **Seed to Harvest:** 70 to 120 days, depending on the variety

- **Earliest Outdoor Planting:** 1 to 2 weeks before the last frost; you can plant some varieties in zone 9 and up in the fall

- **Watering:** water regularly without saturating the soil

RADISH

Radishes taste better when they are grown in cool weather. Once the temperature goes above 65 degrees Fahrenheit, they develop a spicier taste.

- **Growing Seasons:** spring, fall
- **Spacing:** 3 to 4 inches apart

- **Seed to Harvest:** 30 to 60 days

- **Earliest Outdoor Planting:** early spring once your raised bed can be worked

- **Watering:** 1 inch of water per week

RHUBARB

Rhubarb needs extended temperatures below 40 degrees Fahrenheit. The plants thrive in colder climates and can live up to 15 years. In beds, rhubarb plants should be divided sometime between years 5 and 15, basically when they need to be thinned. Do not eat the leaves—they are toxic. Only eat the stalks.

- **Growing Seasons:** spring, late fall in warmer climates
- **Spacing:** 3 to 4 feet apart
- **Seed to Harvest:** 365 days to maturity
- **Earliest Outdoor Planting:** early spring
- **Watering:** 1 inch of water per week

SPINACH

Harvest young leaves as desired. Once the weather starts to warm, harvest the entire plant.

Use bolt-resistant varieties in warmer climates.

- **Growing Seasons:** fall, spring

- **Spacing:** 4 inches

- **Seed to Harvest:** 30 to 44 days

- **Earliest Outdoor Planting:** early in spring; no need to wait for last frost

- **Watering:** needs 1 to 1½ inches of water per week during the growth cycle

SQUASH

Squash have both male and female flowers on the same plant, so they self-pollinate.

- **Growing Seasons:** early spring to early summer

- **Spacing:** 3 to 4 feet apart

- **Seed to Harvest:** 40 to 55 days

- **Earliest Outdoor Planting:** do not plant until the soil reaches 65 degrees Fahrenheit

- **Watering:** 1 to 2 inches of water per week

SUNFLOWER

Harvest sunflower seeds for your own enjoyment, or leave them for your backyard birds and squirrels.

- **Growing Seasons:** spring, late spring
- **Spacing:** 18 to 24 inches
- **Seed to Harvest:** 70 to 90 days
- **Earliest Outdoor Planting:** after danger of frost
- **Watering:** soil should be moist, but not wet

SWEET PEA

Sweet peas are great for borders and lovely as cut flowers. They are not edible.

- **Growing Seasons:** early spring to summer; in frost-free areas can be sown in fall

- **Spacing:** 3 to 6 inches apart

- **Seed to Harvest:** sweet peas are ornamental flowers that generally bloom within 3 to 4 months after planting

- **Earliest Outdoor Planting:** early spring

- **Watering:** 1 inch of water per week

TOMATO

Most tomatoes will not set (make fruit) when it is below 55 degrees Fahrenheit at night. They prefer 60- to 90-degree temperatures during the day, but temperatures higher than 90 degrees during the day will decrease (or halt) production. Some varieties, such as Celebrity, Oregon Spring, and Bush Beefsteak Tomato, will set at cooler temperatures.

- **Growing Seasons:** April through October, depending on location

- **Spacing:** plant tomato plants 3 feet apart in rows 3 feet apart; in a 4-by-4-foot bed, you can plant a maximum of 4 plants, one in each corner; keep them far enough away from the corner so you can trellis them or use a tomato cage

- **Seed to Harvest:** 65 to 85 days

- **Earliest Outdoor Planting:** after the last frost

- **Watering:** water regularly; irregular watering may cause problems such as blossom end rot; tomatoes need at least 1 inch of water per week

ZUCCHINI

Squash plants have both male and female flowers, so they self-pollinate.

- **Growing Seasons:** spring, late spring
- **Spacing:** 36 inches
- **Seed to Harvest:** 40 to 50 days
- **Earliest Outdoor Planting:** after danger of frost
- **Watering:** needs 1 to 2 inches of water per week during the growth cycle

Chapter 5
Cultivation and Harvesting

Cultivation is the term used to describe tilling, hoeing, planting, turning the soil, loosening the soil, and digging. This is the second step in soil preparation for a garden. The first step is selecting the site for your garden, whether it be a one-acre garden or a six foot square raised bed, and then testing the soil for the proper nutrients.

When selecting a site for your garden, choose a sunny spot over a shady spot because vegetables prefer full sun. Locate the garden near a water source and close to your home, if possible, so harvest of your vegetables is convenient. Do not locate the garden near flowers, shrubs, or trees, as they will compete with the garden for nutrients and water both. Avoid areas with heavy plantings of Johnson grass or Bermuda grass, as these are hard weeds to choke. Outline the area of your garden with bricks, stones, timbers or blocks. Fence this area even before you dig so that rabbits will not be attracted. Remove all debris from the land, sticks, weeds, leaves and rocks. Cover the ground with 2 to 4 mm clear plastic, after saturating the ground with water. Extend the plastic six inches beyond the boundaries of the garden to assure all weeds will be killed. Press the plastic to the soil and anchor with bricks, stones and timbers to prevent the plastic from flying in the wind. After six weeks, you can remove the plastic sheeting and prepare the soil. All the weeds and pests should be dead.

In the spring, as soon as the ground is warm and the soil mostly dry, is the time to prepare the soil for planting. Plants need aeration and proper drainage, so turning the soil is necessary to loosen the impacted dirt around the roots and to allow water to flow freely through the root systems. To test your soil for moisture content, pick up a ball of soil and roll it in your hand. Drop the ball to the ground. If the ball holds its shape, it is too moist, check the next day. If the ball is crumbly and dry, water your ground and check the next day. If the ball drops into smaller pieces but not dusty pieces, you are ready to dig.

Dig your ground to a minimum of eight inches. This depth is necessary for a strong root system. A tiller will reach to this depth, as will a tractor or disc. Digging by hand is labor intensive, but also free and good exercise. Consider double-digging to a depth of twenty-four inches. This is time consuming and exhausting, but your garden will produce quadruple the yield of an eight-inch depth plot of land. Double digging cannot be done mechanically but must be done by hand, with a shovel and a fork.

Begin by testing your soil for the pH level, the test for acid and alkaline in the soil. The optimum pH level is between 6.1 and 7.9 pH. Too acidic is below 6.0, too alkaline is above 8.0. Depending on the results of the soil test is the proper combination of nutrients to add to the soil. For example, if your soil is too acidic, you need to add limestone or hardwood ashes to the soil. To raise the acidic level, you need to add finely ground agricultural-grade lime at the rate of a minimum of 3 pounds per 100 square feet. Hardwood ash can be applied at the level, and a mixture of the two is the best additive.

If the soil is too alkaline, you need to add a one-inch layer of peat moss or 2 pounds of agricultural gypsum per 100 square feet, to lower it one point on the pH scale. Nitrogen, phosphorous, and potassium, as well as trace elements, all need to be balanced also. A good organic fertilizer or a compost heap will usually be sufficient to supplement the garden soil. Apply compost to the depth of one to three inches and turn into the soil before beginning the planting season.

Harvesting Your Crops

When to harvest vegetables for the optimum flavor and yield:

- Asparagus: harvest three years after planting. Snap at the soil line, they should be six to eight inches in length, but the heads should not be open. Length of harvest: six weeks.
- Avocados, ripe summer to winter in Florida, fall to spring in California.
- Beans (green and snap): harvest the beans when they are about one fourth developed, if allowed to fully develop it will decrease their yield.
- Beans (Lima): harvest when fully developed and beans are green.
- Beets: harvest the bulb when it is 2 inches in diameter.
- Broccoli: harvest when head is fully developed, cut six inches below head.
- Brussels sprouts: harvest them when 1 ½ inches wide by twisting

the heads off the stems.

- Cabbage:harvest when heads are solid but do not allow them to split, cut just beneath the head.
- •Carrots:harvest when carrots are no more than one inch in diameter, but smaller is better, as carrots will toughen as they thicken.
- •Cauliflower:harvest when heads are full and white.
- •Celery: cut celery stems when ten to twelve inches tall.
- •Cucumbers:if using cucumber to make sweet pickles, cut them at 2 inches long, if using cucumbers for dill pickles, cut them at 4 inches maximum, if slicing cucumbers for the dinner table, cut them at 6 inches. Gather daily.
- •Eggplant: harvest eggplant fruits when black or purple and firm.
- •Lettuce: harvest the outer leaves at 4 to 6 inches long, leave the inner leaves for more yield.
- •Okra: ripe and ready to pick at three inches long.
- •Onions: depends upon type and variety of onion, harvest storage onions at two inches in diameter and before a hard frost.
- •Peas: harvest peas at full development when pods are full and feel tender to the touch.
- •Pod peas: like Spring Peas, harvest at half development when peas are small and soft.
- •Peanuts: harvest when pods are yellow and before the first frost.
- •Pepper (green): harvest when fully ripened firm peppers, and dark green in color.
- •Pepper (red): allow to ripen two to three weeks longer after greening, and pull when red or yellow in color.
- •Potatoes: harvest when fully grown at three inches or more; for new potatoes, harvest whenever ready to eat after one inch in diameter.
- •Pumpkins: harvest when pumpkin is fully orange and skin is hard to the touch.
- •Radishes (American): harvest radishes at one to one and a half

inches around.

- •Rhubarb: harvest after second year of planting, pull at root to one side and cut.
- •Rutabaga or turnips: harvest after ripe and when bulb is two to three inches in diameter.
- •Spinach: harvest the leaves at no more than 4 inches. They will grow more leaves as long as the root is intact.
- •Squash (summer): harvest at 4 inches when skin is ripe.
- •Squash (winter): harvest when outer skin is hard and not easily marred with a fingernail.
- •Sweet corn: harvest when kernels are filled with milk, silks will be brown.
- •Sweet potato: harvest when sweet potato is 4 inches in length, harvest before the frost.
- •Tomatoes: pick tomatoes when red and firm.
- When to harvest fruits for the optimum flavor and yield:
- •Apples: ripe July to November.
- •Apricots: ripe May to June.
- •Bananas: ripe late summer to fall.
- •Blueberries: ripe 60-80 days after full bloom.
- •Cherries: ripe May to July.
- •Citrus fruit: ripe year round in warm climates.
- •Figs: ripe June and July.
- •Gooseberries: ripe late spring and early summer.
- •Guavas: Fall in California, June through October in Florida.
- •Loquats: February to May in Florida, March to June in California.
- •Muskmelon: harvest when stem cracks at base.
- •Mangoes: May to September in Florida, fall to winter in California.
- •Nectarines: as early as April to September.
- •Olives: ripe in the fall.

- •Papayas: in California 8 months after blooms, in Florida, 4 months after blooms.
- •Peaches: ripe April to September.
- •Pears: ripe July to October.
- •Persimmons: ripe late fall to early winter.
- •Plums: ripe June to August.
- •Pomegranates: ripe when fully dark hued.
- •Raspberries: ripe early summer to fall.
- •Quince: ripe in the fall.
- •Watermelon: harvest at full size when rind is yellow on the ground.

Chapter 6
How to Grow any Plants

Veggies give crucial nourishment into your body and also are a portion of the healthy diet plan and way of life. Specific veggies might be eaten uncooked -- just as salads whereas some others will need to get cooked.Whatever manner we have veggies, they all truly are yummy and offer enormous health advantages.

It's far more satisfying to raise your veggies and utilize them into your ordinary cooking!Homegrown veggies maybe not just taste delicious but are even fitter compared to the crops that are commercially grown. If you're health-conscious, absolutely nothing works a lot better than the usual full bowl of freshly prepared salad out of homegrown plants and herbs.

Plants could be Perennial, Annual, or Biennial. Perennial crops endure for at least a couple of decades ago. Annual vegetation germinate blossom and perish within a season or two over this entire year.

Biennial vegetation requires a long time to finish their entire life span.

Listing of Vegetables Can Be Grown Indoors Productively

Salad greens

Spinach -- germination period is just 6 to 12 times; is now just a winter season annual harvest water-cress -- seed germination does occur in seven to fourteen times; is now really a continuing harvest Arugula -- germinates per week; is the two continuing and yearly Mustard -- germinates in 5 to ten times; special seed species predominate every day! Lettuce -- requires 2 weeks to germinate; is still a temperate yearly or biennial.

Herbs

Dill -- germinates at per week period; is still a Yearly pill Coriander -- germination period is generally ten times; is now a Yearly herb Basil -- germinates in 6 to Ten times; is still a Yearly herb Chamomile -- seed germination period is 7 to 14 times; is continuing but increased since yearly Steak -- needs Fortnight or longer to its first g to seem; is continuing Mint -- germination period 7 to Fortnight; is continuing Tarragon -- germinates in 7 to 14 times; you Are Unable to increase French Tarragon out of seeds Sage --

germinates at a Couple of months; backyard blossom or common blossom is continuing Thyme -- may endure 3 to 4 months and occasionally over per month; will be continuing.

PLANT MIXTURES

If you intend to cultivate more than one harvest at one moment, then there are distinct mixes you may like to abide by along with Distinct plants possess similar demands nutrient conditions, germination period, progress phases, etc. Growing this sort of plant together might assist you to produce plants of far better quality and amount.

Here's a list of plants which possess similar demands:

Tomatoes

Tomatoes are the absolute most widely used vegetable in this type of gardening. Most commercially developed berries belong to the indeterminate type. In the event you would like to cultivate smaller berries to fit your area needs, then decide on seeds so.

Tomatoes mature in just about any type of Raised Bed technique; however, a Drip process would be your very best. Seed germination period is just 3 to 6 weeks; also, it'll simply take one hundred days until you may realize your tomato crops endure veggies; however, they often persist in creating veggies for your year.Similar plants: Peppers and Cucumbers.

Lettuce

An All-Time favored amongst Raised Bed farmers. Leaf lettuce can be a far greater choice compared to thoughts carrot.

Nutrient Film process might be your optimal/optimally strategy to cultivate Lettuce; otherwise, you might even increase it into an Ebb and circulation or trickle system.

Lettuce seeds germinate in 4 weeks to 2 days also certainly will be chosen at 3-5 to 4-5 times, so to keep up a constant source of seed, lettuce them just about every day or two.

Much like plants: Spinach, Basil, and foliage plants.

Carrots

Carrot can be an origin crop that grows nicely in Perlite; thus will almost any additional origin harvest such as radish and beets.

Roots crops take a huge expansion mattress to raise and acquire totally.

It requires about 6 to ten weeks to allow its seeds germinate and 2.5 to a couple of weeks to crop.

Much like plants: Beets, Leeks, Radish.

Cucumber

Cucumbers are long-lasting plants and keep steadily to give up fruits to a few weeks.European cinema types are simpler to cultivate in raised beds. Cucumbers need to have considerable distance and encouragement to cultivate.

Basil

Basil is an herb that develops involving 12 to 18 inches tall. Buds and blossoms have to be pruned frequently to motivate continuing development.

It requires about 6 to ten weeks to its Basil seeds to germinate and certainly will create refreshing leaves for three weeks to 4 weeks. After three weeks to 4 weeks, the older chamomile plant has to have been substituted using a fresh 1.

Similar plants: Spinach and Lettuce

Beans

You can harvest substantial returns from bean blossoms. An Ebb and Flow process works nicely with Perlite or expanded clay pellets. Seed germination normally takes about 3 to 2 days; also, you may begin harvesting within six weeks to fourteen days. You may keep on opting for three days to 4 weeks.

Peppers

Peppers can be found in the number of colors and tastes. You may grow both equally sweet and hot peppers. Utilize a trickle machine or an Ebb and Flow process to cultivate those veggies. Pepper vegetation expands tall -- with an increasing content that gives the essential service is necessary; you may utilize rock-wool for seed germination and after utilize Perlite blended with Vermiculite and nice gravel.

It requires 10 to fourteen weeks for seed germination, and you'll be able to harvest from the 4th calendar month.

Much like plants: Tomatoes and Cucumbers.

Spinach

Spinach develops nicely within an NFT Process or an Ebb and Flow Technique. You may utilize rock-wool for seed germination; maintenance has to be chosen to present enough escalating distance for all these plants differently you hazard racking them.The common space enabled between 2 vegetation is 20 sq. Inches.

Seed germination takes 6 to 1-2 weeks, and also the very first crop begins just from the conclusion of 2nd calendar month (approx. fifty to sixty times).

Much like plants: Basil, Lettuce.

Growing Herbs: The Raised Bed Way

Just about everyone people would want the notion of using freshly juiced herbs in cooking. Though you always have the option to grow these herbaceous plants in dirt, you're able to benefit from a much healthier herb if grown in raised beds.

Basil

The most effective system to disperse growth is NFT -- move the seedlings into NFT when seedlings are 1 or 2 inches. Seed germination takes 7days; supply a projection of 9 to 12 inches between plants. You can utilize vermiculite, soil-less combinations, rock-wool, and coco-peat. Basil thrives and continues to rise at considerable sunshine and requires 1-1 hours. Don't crop ginger on short days as it's vulnerable to ailments. The most typical reasons for the illness are in Aphids and Pythium.USDA hardiness isn't appropriate to Basil.

Chamomile

Chamomile is a yearly herb that's small white blossoms; those blossoms are inserted to tea to provide a different flavor and cause medicinal properties. Chamomile seeds need light to germinate and take 7 to 2 weeks for germination. These herbaceous plants add to a height of 20 to 30 inches and then perform nicely with a diameter of 6 inches between plants. Potential bugs are Aphids and Mealy bugs. USDA Hardiness is annual.

Chervil

This herb is owned by the Parsley family and can be chiefly employed as a culinary herb. This herb thrives under cool temperatures (700 to 750 F); avoid exposing it to sunlight. Germination period for Chervil is just about per week transplant the seedlings to NFT once the very first true leaves appear.Spacing between plants has to be kept at 1 inch, and then you'll be able to start to harvest at monthly. Chervil is more likely to Aphids, especially during hot days.

Cilantro

Cilantro or Coriander is one of the Parsley family; cilantro tastes like parsley but having a citrus twist. These plants give seeds that can be employed in various color combinations, liquors, and confectioneries. The leaves could be applied as a culinary herb. Cilantro climbs well in the sun; you could utilize fluorescent lights or HID lighting fixtures.Seed germination normally takes approximately ten weeks as well as the plant could grow as many as two feet tall.Pests that could strike cilantro are Aphids, whitefly, mites, and thrips.

Dill

Dill, too, is one of the Parsley family and is still an annual / supplement. Dill seeds are traditionally found in pickles along with also the herb itself is traditionally employed as a culinary taste enhancer. All these plants usually reach a height of 24 to 36 inches and have to be dispersed 12 to 15 inches apart. It requires approximately ten weeks for your seeds to germinate and the plant grows well in sunlight. Employing HID lights may perform just fine inside. Care has to be used never to Over Water Dill plants; USDA hardiness isn't related to Dill. Also, it might be affected by powdery mildew and aphids.

Lavender

A flowering plant which is one of the mint family, lavender flowers, if dried out a pleasing odor; those blossoms are frequently utilized in aromatherapy perfumes and oils. Lavender grows to a height of 18 inches; the spacing needs to have been 20 to 24 inches between plants. Seed germination may choose between 10 to 28 days.Lavender needs enough sun; mimic the lighting utilizing HID lights. Lavender might be assaulted by white-fly, spider mites, mealy scales, and bugs.

Lemon Balm

This goes back to the mint family and is popularly famous for its soothing properties.It's regarded that a 'soothing herb.' Lemon Balm develops well under partial sun and propagates through plants and seeds.Seed germination takes five days and 3 to 30 days to root development.Transplant the seedlings when they're approximately 2 inches tall.Lemon Balm is allergic to White-fly assault, Spider Mite, and Thrip.

Marjoram

All these are perennial herbaceous plants grown as annuals; you will find two varieties -- sweet and wild. Sweet Marjoram is traditionally employed as a culinary herb. It grows to a height up to 3-6 inches, and also the spacing between plants needs to have been 15 to 18 inches. Germination period is 10 to 15 days; those herbaceous plants grow well under the sun. Deficiency of light or bad illumination structures can lead the plant to die to fungal diseases.Marjoram is allergic to many different fungal diseases and white-fly strikes.

Chapter 7
Benefits of a Raised Bed Garden

Raised bed gardens are ideal if you have less than ideal soil conditions or very little space. They typically are made from built up soil, or even framed with wood- untreated, of course- or other materials. You can purchase the materials to make your own, or you can get a pre-made, boxed one if you think that'll make it any easier to get started.

You can get a much higher crop yield in a much smaller area. Raised beds look great and allow much easier access to the plants. They offer an extended growing season due to soil conditions. With just a little bit of planning, you can be sure that your raised bed garden will yield many crops.

Having a raised bed garden makes gardening much less hassle and work. There are many benefits to raised bed gardening. Here are nine benefits to raised gardening.

First of all, a raised bed garden will save your back. You don't have to bend over nearly as far to reach plants in raised beds, which will reduce your back strain. Since you have less potential for pain and much easier access to your plants, you will be able to better enjoy planting, tending, and even harvesting your raised bed garden.

Tip: Make sure that you build your raised bed gardens at least 1 foot tall. If the walls are just below waist level, you can sit on the edge to tend and harvest, which means no bending at all!

The second benefit to raised bed gardens is your plants will grow much longer in raised bed. Typically, the soil in raised bed will warm much earlier in spring than the ground. Also, it dries out much faster, so you can plant your cool-season crops much sooner, which will extend the growing season and your choices for vegetable crops.

Tip: in order to extend the gardening season for raised bed, you can fashion canopies over your beds and place plastic on them. This will hold the cold in and therefore help you get extra growing time in spring and fall.

The third benefit is that you can keep your feet clean. You can have mulch on the paths between your raised bed and your feet stay clean no matter how wet the weather is. Also, since you're not walking on the beds themselves, you will be able to run out and grab a handful of fresh herbs without having to worry about the soil being compacted.

The fourth benefit to a raised bed garden is that you can overcome your bad soil. If you have clay or sandy soil, it can be quite difficult to raise plants in. However, if you have a raised bed garden, you can purchase top quality topsoil and get over that bad soil. When you have soil that is rich in nutrients, then your plants will struggle less and you will have less frustration. In order to keep your raised bed garden soil healthy, you will need to add compost and other organic material on a regular basis.

The fifth benefit of a raised bed garden is that weeds are reduced. Simply fill your raised bed with fresh soil, cover the surface with about an inch of mulch. This will reduce weeds as well as preserve moisture in your raised garden bed.

The sixth benefit of a raised bed garden is that you can stop grass from invading your crops. The grass on your lawn has a root system that spreads and can get into and overtake a standard vegetable garden. However, when you have raised bed, the grass can't spread to them.

The seventh benefit to raised bed gardens is that pests are stopped. Though they can still get in, you can stop them by building your raised bed just a bit taller to discourage them from getting in.

The eighth benefit of raised bed gardening is that you can make your garden much nicer. You can set up a group of raised beds in a neat pattern or nice, neat rows to get a raised bed garden that is visually appealing.

The ninth and final benefit that we will discuss is that you will never have to till again with a raised bed garden. When you have a traditional garden, in order to create a healthy environment or your earthworms and microorganisms, you must till the ground. This aerates the soil and allows it to breathe. Since there is no one walking on the raised beds, the soil doesn't get compacted, so you won't need to till the ground.

So, as you see, raised bed gardens offer many benefits, from saving your back to saving your plants from being choked out by pests or weeds. Overall, raised bed gardening is a great choice when you want to raise your own food.

Why Should I Use Raised Bed Gardening?

Sometimes called boxed gardening or garden boxes, you need raised garden beds if you're planning to grow vegetable and fruit plots. When you just try to plant fruits and vegetables, even flowers, in your garden without any boxes, weeds may just grow near them. Of course, this means that they would not be protected from soil compaction, and from being drained of nutrients by the said weeds.

The Benefits

More so, raised garden beds prove to be important when it comes to protecting plants from certain pests, such as snails or slugs, for example, and in making sure that plants get equal amounts of water and humidity. This is because soil that's placed in a closed spot is warmer than soil that's just on the ground.

Meanwhile, the bottoms of raised garden beds are actually open—which means that water could easily be absorbed by the roots, as opposed to being absorbed by the stems, which would do nothing good for the plants. This way, the plants would get the nutrients that they need—without any blockage!

Chapter 8
Tips for growing healthy plants

As it has been stated before, plants that are healthy are less susceptible to diseases and pests than those that are less healthy. I try to keep my plants as healthy as possible to help them be able to fight diseases better. Keeping your plants healthy will help to boost their immune system. Here are a few tips that can be employed to ensure that your plants stay healthy and are able to protect themselves diseases.

1. Ensure that they are well fed and watered.

2. Build and environment in the garden that will conducive enough for beneficial insects and predators. This can encourage wildlife that will help dispel smaller pest. For example ladybugs and lace wigs feed on aphids and birds and hedgehogs feed on slugs.

3. You can employ biological controls such as nematodes which can be used to combat snails on hosts or vine weevil in containers.

4. Select plant species that more resistant to certain diseases e.g. some carrot species are more resistant to carrot fly than others.

5. I am in the league of those farmers who believe that growing some plants close to others can have mutual benefits for both of the plants. This is popularly known as companion planting. For example, carrot and onion being planted together can provide both of the plants with some benefits. Onion fly are deterred by the smell of carrots and so is carrot fly deterred by the smell of onion.

6. Grow your plants spaciously so that air will be able to circulate effectively around the raised bed. I make use of a small rake to clear away any fallen leaves or rotting fruits from the floor. You should be vigilant and remove any infected material from the plant as soon as you can spot it.

Handling Pests

Pests are a staple of gardens or farms, and your raised bed will not be an exception. All you can do is just to get yourself prepared for them whenever they decide to manifest themselves. You should be more careful and take preventive measures especially if you want to grow delicious fruits or fresh vegetables. These are the kind of plants that pests are most attracted to.

You can apply some chemical controls to do away with the invasion of these pests, some of them which are very effective. But there are some other non-chemical methods of pest control that you can employ to control pest, most of which won't have any side effects on the garden.

Here are some of the most common pest that attack gardens

1.Slugs

These pests are very slow but steady vegetable 'munchers', and if care is not taken, the entire crop can be wiped out in a few nights. The elevation that comes with raised beds will mean that fewer of these slugs will be able to find their way to the garden, but this does not entirely stop them.

Slugs are naturally slow pests and you can easily spot some of them lying at the base of the raised bed trying to get to the top of the garden. You can pick them up and dispose them however that fits you.

There are two non-chemical methods I employ to help me with slug control. The first is to make a beer or sugary solution trap. Slugs are attracted to that kind of thing. Place the solution in a container that has been sunk into the ground so that the top is level with the ground. Slugs will gather into the container and feed on the solution and they will be unable to get out until you arrive.

The second is to scatter orange peels around the bases of the garden to attract them. Then you come and pick them up and dispose.

2.Birds

Birds play an important role in protecting the garden from the invasion of pest, but nevertheless, they still take out them to consume some of the plants whenever they can. For example, pigeons are known to love cabbages and sprouts. Most other birds will love to devour some ripe fruits.

One way to keep your plants secured and protected from birds is to protect them with a bird net and using a raised bed makes it easier construct. You can make a protective cage by simply digging in some bamboo sticks into the ground around the raised bed. Then use a net to cover it until every part of the bed has been protected.

3.Aphids

They can be found on the shoot and leaves of plants. One way in which I control their invasion is by releasing ladybug or lacewing larvae around the plants that they have attacked. The larvae feed on the aphids.

4.Carrot Fly

These flies are particularly attracted to the smell of carrot. You can prevent their attack by growing resistant carrot species or cover the growing carrot with a fine mesh to keep off the tiny flies.

5.Beetles

They can feed on you plants no matter how small and immature they are. You can make use of Milky spore to eliminate the grubs (their larvae form).

6.Rodents

These ones feed on the seeds you have just planted out, mostly peas or beans. They also won't hesitate to feed on fruits and corn seeds.

You can get rids of them by covering the raised bed with wire nets or by making use of poisons. Consult your local pest control company for the best rodent poison that won't affect the plants.

Chapter 9
Planting and Maintaining Crops in Raised Bed Gardens

Once you have already built your raised beds, prepared the soil, and selected the crops that you want to grow, you can start planting them. There are certain steps that you need to take to plant the crops properly and maintain them.

Here are the proper ways to plant your crops and help them grow healthy:

Spacing between Plants

You can adhere to the typical garden plant spacing, which is in rows, or you might choose the square foot gardening that helps you use most of your space. This is done through marking off the garden bed in 12-inch square sections. Then you can start planting your seeds, one type of plant for each square. You can make a personalized diagram of your beds, so you know which plants you have planted in every square.

Block planting is also recommended with proper spacing between plants to achieve better plant production. For large plants like tomatoes or squash, you will have to make 24-inch centers. If you are trying to grow medium-sized crops like peas, onions, and beans, you'll need to plant them 4 to 6 inches apart. If your garden is for small crops like root crops and green leafy vegetables, you'll simply need to scatter the seeds over a small section on your garden's soil.

Position Plants Strategically

It is recommended that you put plants that need less care in the middle part of the bed and those that require more care on the edges. If only one side of your raised bed garden can be reached by sunlight, you need to do two things. Place the smaller ones toward the southern part and the taller plants on the northern part. If you are planting cucumbers, position them near the edge of the bed to allow them to trail over the side.

Determine the Right Depth

It is necessary to determine the right depth for the crop that you are trying to grow. To begin, you have to know that a minimum of 6 inches deep is necessary for most vegetables to grow well above ground. For root vegetables, a depth of 10 to 12 inches is necessary. However, there are also crops that don't need to be covered with thick soil. If you are planting lettuce, you need to make a one-half inch deep furrow before sprinkling the seeds into every hole. You may then sprinkle a thin layer of soil to cover the lettuce seeds. If you are planting carrots, cover the seeds with fine-textured potting soil.

Practice Companion Planting

Just like other gardening methods, you can also take advantage of companion planting to reduce the risk of pest infestation. Allow compatible plants to grow close together and benefit from one another. You can plant beans with corn to increase nitrogen supply or with borage to repel worms in tomatoes. You can also grow peppers with spinach in between. This will allow the peppers to provide shade to the spinach and extend its picking season to make it more delicious.

However, you need to remember that there are crop combinations you need to avoid, such as corn and tomatoes. These crops attract the same pest, such as corn earworms or tomato fruit worm.

Water and Mulch Your Garden after Planting

After planting your crop, nourish it with adequate amounts of water. Makes sure that the soil is only moistened, not drenched. You also need to mulch your garden with wood chips, leaves, straw, or grass clippings to keep the soil moist and prevent weeds.

Maintaining Your Raised Bed Garden

When it comes to maintaining your raised bed garden, if you have mixed your soil well, then it may retain water better. Therefore, you don't need to keep watering it. You just need to allow the top inch of the soil to dry before you water it again. You can also dig down 6 inches every now and then to check how your garden soil has been retaining water or moisture.

There are crops that require more soil as they are growing. For instance, if you are growing asparagus, you need to add more soil to the furrows as the crop starts growing. The furrows should be filled and be in the same soil level of the raised bed. This will satisfy the plant's growing needs and help it grow normally.

Even if you choose the best garden soil, it will still need constant rejuvenation, so fertilizers need to be used. For instance, you can add a foliar fertilizer, which ensures that your plant gets the right nutrients without having to deplete the soil with all its nutrients. You should also rotate your vegetable crop over a four-year cycle to prevent soil depletion from happening. At the same time, you prevent diseases or pests from getting into your vegetable crops.

Always remember that the health and productivity of your crops largely depend on how you plant and grow them. Plant them properly and ensure that they are getting the nutrients they need to survive and grow healthy.

High-Yielding Garden: The Secrets

You probably will not believe me if I tell you that it is quite possible to harvest almost a half-ton of beautiful, tasty organic veggies from a fifteen by twenty-foot garden plot. What if I tell you that you can get one hundred pounds of lush tomatoes from a four by twenty-four-foot plot or twenty pounds of crunchy carrots from only twenty-four square feet? Yes, these unbelievable yields can certainly be achieved, and it is easier than you imagined. For your garden to be so super productive, all you have to do is work out the right strategies for your specific circumstances.

I will now provide you with seven strategies for high yielding vegetable gardening. These are all tried and tested methods from experienced super productive gardeners who know how to use the space in their gardens optimally.

1.Build up Rich Soil

The quality of your soil is by far the most important contributing factor to productivity. All the expert gardeners agree on this.Therefore, to start off, you need deep soil, rich in organic matter to encourage extensive, healthy root systems that are then able to get to all the water and nutrients. A strong root system in the soil will result in extra productive plant growth outside the soil.

What is the fastest and easiest manner to obtain such a deep fertile soil? Plant your vegetables in raised beds. Plants in rows on the ground will yield four times less than those planted in the same space in raised beds gardens. This is firstly due to the efficient use of space; no space is wasted on paths between rows. Secondly, the rich, loose soil in raised beds will increase the productivity of your plants and help them to grow to their full potential.

By the way, it has been proven that you will also save lots of time if you grow your veggies in raised beds. A researcher wrote down how many hours he spent planting and maintaining his thirty by thirty foot garden in raised beds. He was astounded to find that he only had to spend twenty-seven hours during a five-month season from May to October. On top of this, his harvest during these five months came to a thousand nine hundred pounds of all kinds of fresh veggies! He calculated that he produced enough crops for a family of three for an entire year.

You may well ask how this is possible. Well, the plants in raised bed gardens are planted close together with the result that they prevent weeds from growing, and therefore you spend a lot less time fighting these unwelcome intruders. Your garden is also less spread out, which makes fertilizing, harvesting, and watering a lot more efficient.

2. Rounded Out Beds

The surface shape of the beds will also make some difference. For example, a bed with a width of five foot along its frame, if rounded on top into a gentle arch, will mean that you now have an extra surface of a foot across for planting your seedlings.Maybe it does not sound like so much, but when you multiply this number with the length of the bed, you will realize what a difference it will make to your total planting area.

The longer the bed, the more the increase in planting space will amount to if you round the top surface. Therefore, if your bed is twenty foot in length, you can increase the area from a hundred to hundred and twenty square feet. A twenty percent gain can make a tremendous difference when you look at the total output you can obtain from this.

The crops that are best suited to this kind of beds are greens like lettuce and spinach; they can be planted all along the edges.

3.How to Space Smartly

In order to obtain the highest yield possible from every bed, you have to arrange the plants in the best space-saving arrangement. Rows or square patterns do not work well in this regard. Using triangles to stagger your plants will enable you to fit in ten to fourteen more vegetable plants in a bed.

However, there are some plants that do not like to be crowded; they will not be able to grow to their optimum size if they are too close together. It is not always the number of plants per square foot that will yield the most. One research gardener found that his romaine lettuces actually produced more weight-wise when he planted them ten inches apart instead of eight inches like previously.

Plants that are too tightly spaced together may experience stress, and they will end up being more prone to disease and susceptible to attacks by insects.

Chapter 10
Advantages of Raised Bed Gardening

Some of the major benefits that come with raised bed gardening can be found below, which might explain why this form of gardening has become so popular.

Better Soil Management

One of the major benefits of raised bed gardening is that it allows for better soil management and you do not need to be concerned if your soil is of poor quality. You are more in control of the environment in which you grow vegetables and other plants because this method of gardening allows you to prepare your own high quality soil mix for the raised bed.This way of gardening is especially beneficial if native garden soil is of poor quality and there are soil fertility problems on the land.It is also beneficial if the soil is of heavy clay or if gardening in areas where the soil is polluted or has high salinity.Successful gardening and a fertile soil go hand in hand.You cannot have one without the other. A fertile soil, rich in available plant-food, is essential to grow healthy vegetables if they are to produce a good harvest, which we can all agree, is the main purpose of our gardening efforts.Therefore, a plant must get certain nutrients from the soil in which it is to grow, otherwise it will fail to thrive and reach maturity.Essential plant-food includes nitrogen, phosphoric acid potash and lime, to some extent, and various other chemical elements. When there is poor soil, the plant-food in the soil may be chemically unavailable or not available in sufficient amounts for growing plants. Raised bed gardening allows you to create your own high quality soil mix to fill the bed to ensure that your plants get sufficient nutrients to grow and to remain healthy and productive.Using a special soil mix in a raised bed makes the soil light, well drained, rich in nutrients and easily workable.This enables plants to get established quicker because it's easier for moisture to reach the roots of the plants. Their roots can breathe easier and therefore get a better hold in the soil to create a strong root system. The result will be a garden full of thriving, healthy, productive plants.

Improved Drainage

A waterlogged soil is useless for growing crops.A well-drained soil is required to grow healthy plants.The composition of the soil mix allows for improved drainage, allowing excess water to drain away so that plants are not waterlogged.The well-being of soil and plants requires that the level of surplus water caused by heavy rainfall must go a long way below the surface.Therefore, excess water must be able to drain away to allow the soil to admit air freely.The presence of air in the soil is essential to the changes in the soil that makes plant-food available to growing crops.

Easier Access to Gardening Areas

Raised bed gardening is a convenient way of gardening because it allows for easier access to gardening areas. Because the beds are raised off the ground it's not necessary to bend down as far to tend the garden and the need to bend over is very much reduced.Fatigue that is often caused by the physical effort of gardening and injury to knees and back that can be caused by bending is reduced. The raised bed method is particularly convenient for those who find it difficult to do traditional ground gardening. This way of gardening is therefore ideal for anyone who is unable to reach down to the ground, such as the elderly, wheelchair or cane users or anyone with a bad back.A raised bed can be raised off the ground at a height to suit the gardener's needs. Therefore, gardening can be done in waist high raised beds, which means it's not necessary to reach down to tend the garden.A raised bed can also be built on a surface, such as a raised platform in the most convenient place to make gardening easily accessible.

However, if the raised bed is to be built on an elevated surface, such as a raised platform, you should ensure that the surface is very stable and strong enough to bear the weight of the bed, to avoid accidents.

No Tilling Required

It's not necessary to till the soil to keep it cultivated in a raised bed because the soil is protected from foot traffic.Tilling is normally necessary in traditional ground gardening when the soil is compacted due to it being stepped on or is compacted by other means.If the raised bed garden is designed properly, so that the whole garden area is easily accessible, it will not be necessary to step on the soil, so it will not become compacted.It's easier for plants to establish a strong root system in the loose soil so they will get off to a good start. There will be much less weeds because it's harder for weed seeds to get into the garden, since it is raised off the ground.

Conserves Water

The special soil mix helps the soil to retain more moisture so a raised bed garden needs less water and does not need to be watered as often as a traditional garden that is reliant on native soil, watering the plants by hand, as opposed to using a hose, will save water and the plants will also benefit as the water can be directed at their roots and not wasted.Hand watering also protects young plants from damage by heavy watering and protects the soil cover in seedbeds.Building your raised bed next to your water source will of course also save time in watering the garden. Less watering means you will be able to conserve water and save money on your water bill, looking after your raised bed garden will therefore be easier and less time consuming and has the added advantage of being an economical way of gardening.

Extended Growing Season

Gardening in raised beds allows for a longer growing season. A raised bed garden will warm up faster since it is raised above the ground. The soil will also remain warm for much longer as it is enclosed within a restricted space.Building your raised bed in a sunny spot will also help to warm the soil faster and it will catch more heat and light in the colder months of spring. This will give your plants a head start in the growing season, as you will be able to start seeds off or set young plants off outdoor earlier. This is particularly beneficial if you live in a cold climate. Plants grown in raised beds usually remain productive for longer into the growing season, which means you will have more delicious fresh produce to enjoy.

Organizing Plants to Cater for Their Needs

Raised bed gardening allows you to more easily organize your plants so that you can cater for their individual needs.The ability to prepare your own soil mix allows you to create the right growing environment to suit different type of plants.For instance, some plants need a highly acidic soil.The soil can be specially prepared for these types of plants to the right pH balance. Also, crops with the similar soil requirements, such as that requiring well-drained or well-fertilized soil, can be planted together in one bed. Plants with different soil requirements such as tomatoes and potatoes can be grown in different beds.Tomatoes are prolific vine plants, so require a lot of room to grow. On the other hand, potatoes are deep-rooted plants that require a deep bed with at least 12 inches of good quality soil.

Improved Visibility

The raised soil level of a raised bed gives a better view of the plants in the garden.This is useful because the beds are easier to work and allows you to take better care of your plants and vegetables.It is easier to see weeds and spot garden pests like slugs and snails that can harm your plants. Slugs and snails can easily be removed or eradicated.It's much easier and effective to treat the soil in a concentrated space to get rid garden pests and their eggs.Similarly, it's much easier to spot attacks on your plants from insects and bacteria or fungal attacks that can have a detrimental effect on the health of plants. Any attacks on your plants can also be easily treated.The affected bed can be treated and quarantined by using a protective mesh cover to help to confine the problem to that bed.

Protecting your Plants

A raised bed garden makes it easier to protect your crops from bad weather, birds and flying insects that can be destructive to plants.Plastic sheeting can be used to cover the bed at night to provide frost protection in spring and against the wind and rain in cooler seasons.Bird netting can be used to guard against birds eating or destroying crops. A series of wooden posts or other suitable material can be inserted around the perimeter of the raised bed on which to drape the plastic sheeting or bird netting.

Chapter 11
Common Mistakes to Avoid

If you have been paying attention throughout the book then a lot of what you read in this chapter will be information that you encountered before. This is because the book is written to give you all the information you need to garden like a pro. Simply put, you have already learned the right way to plan and care for a raised bed garden. When you learn the right way, you avoid making mistakes by acting on assumption and instead act with knowledge and comprehension.

Overwatering Your Plants

This is the last chance there is to reinforce the idea that it is better for your plants to be too dry than too wet. While plants need plenty of water, too much water is the deadliest thing of all. It gets into the soil around the roots and prevents them from sucking in oxygen. The roots will blacken and die. They go from having a solid texture almost like a piece of string and instead start to feel slimy and gross.

So the best way to avoid this tragic experience is to avoid overwatering your plants. Always give the finger test before watering and if you are unsure then be cautious and wait a day. It only takes a moment but it can save you the work of removing and replanting your crops. Plants will begin to wilt when they are overly thirsty and this can be a sign to water them. But make sure this wilting isn't just due to the noonday sun. Some plants will wilt in order to protect themselves from the hottest temperatures of the day. Once the sun starts to set, they will stop wilting.

Skipping Out on Maintenance

Maintenance is so important. This another one of those mistakes that happens often enough to be embarrassing. There is simply no excuse for leaving your garden completely untended to. When you do this you are choosing to completely ignore any signs of danger that you might have been able to catch early.

The biggest problems with untended beds are weeds and dead plant matter. Weeds will completely take over a raised garden bed if you don't catch them early. Skipping out on maintenance for half a week could lead to an infestation you are unable to beat without replacing the soil. Weeds that get out of hand will starve out your plants and this will lead to far more leaves dropping off them than normal.

Ignoring the Drainage

When you mix up your own soil, you are doing it to create a quickly draining texture. Raised garden beds drain better due to their elevated positions but you still need to use well-draining soil. Introducing too many plants will block up the soil and slow down the draining, while preventing any one plant from getting enough nutrients. Weeds will also slow down the drainage. But the biggest problem is failing to include drainage holes in the raised bed frame itself.

Using the Wrong Soil

This mixture will work for many plants but not for all of them. You need to do your research on what you are going to grow to see if this soil mixture will work for them. Typically, most of what you want to grow is either going to enjoy this or it will want something with a little more of a sandy texture. More minerals in the soil will increase the speed of drainage but not every plant enjoys a sandy soil.

The disappointing thing with using the wrong soil is that you may not realize it is wrong when you first start using it because it does a decent enough job. You might think that your plants are doing fine, when they are actually smaller than they should be. But when you provide them with a soil that is right, you will notice a major difference in the size and depth of color they take. This is especially true if the soil you have chosen doesn't have enough nutrients in it.

But the other issue with soil is that the right soil last year might not be the right soil a year later. The quality of soil degrades over time, more so if it is reliant on organic components like compost. It is important to pay close attention to your soil. Degrading soil will start to drain much slower. You may need to mix in some more minerals and compost but this can be hard to do after you have planted your raised beds for the year. A good way to get a heads up on this issue is to water your beds before you plant anything. Doing this will let you see if they are draining properly or not. Take a few minutes to also dig through the soil and see if it "feels" right.

Making Your Raised Beds Too Wide

Your raised garden beds, or even those beds in the ground themselves, should never be more than four feet wide. This is done so that you can tend to all of the plants in the bed, including those in the middle that are the hardest to reach. You may believe that you can reach a little further than that and so might make a larger raised garden bed but you will find that once your plants start to come in it gets a lot harder to reach those middle ones than you expected. While they are seeds or seedlings, there is nothing obstructing your view or reach but once foliage starts to grow in it can become like trying to navigate through a miniature jungle.

Remember that length doesn't matter. You can make your beds as long as you want, it is purely about width. However, if you have blocked off one of the long sides of the raised bed by having it up against a house or barn then you will want to go with a slightly thinner design no wider than three feet.

Building Raised Beds Too Close Together

This pairs well with not making your raised garden beds too wide. If you are going to be placing garden beds next to each other then you should make sure there is two feet or so between them. You might be able to get away with a foot and a half but it is better to have a little more space than not enough. The reason we don't make our raised garden beds more than four feet wide is so that we can access all of our plants in order to keep an eye on them and maintain their health. This is the exact same reason that you want to have enough space to be able to easily maneuver between your beds. If you can't properly move around the garden bed then you are effectively cutting off access to an entire side and reducing your ability to properly look after those far away plants.

This is even worse when you consider that the reason this happened is because of a second raised garden bed and this means there are twice as many plants getting neglected. You might really want to squeeze two beds into a small patch of direct sunlight but doing so might put your plants at risk and defeat the whole purpose. In a case like this where there is very limited space to fit two raised garden beds, stick with just one.

Using the Wrong Material

Again, we've already covered the importance of using a safe material when building our raised bed frames but this needs to be stressed again. There are plenty of safe materials that you can use like concrete, stone, bricks, hardwoods, and more. But there are also materials which degrade the quality of the land and the soil. Tires might be an easy way to add some circular imagery to your landscaping but they should only be used for non-edible flowers since they could seep heavy metals into the soil. Then there are downright deadly materials like railway ties, which are so toxic to the land around them that there have been several governments issued warnings against their use in the United States. It is important to make sure that the material you are using isn't going to end up taking a bite out of your or your plants' health.

Poisoning the Growing Environment

This one ties in directly with using unsafe materials. One of the reasons that raised bed gardening is so attractive is the level of control it gives gardeners over the growing environment. While the soil in your backyard might not be healthy at all, you take control of the soil you use in your raised bed garden so that you know it is perfectly safe and healthy.

Another way is to use chemical fertilizers, pesticides, fungicides, or herbicides on your garden. If you don't know what you are spraying on your plants then you won't even know if you are doing something good for them or harmful to them. One of the reasons that organic gardening has been getting so big lately is precisely because organic practices move away from using harmful chemicals. When used on a raised garden bed, the first thing that will get sick is the soil of the raised bed.

While we're discussing this as a beginner mistake, the sad truth is there are many "experts" who make this particular mistake all the time. In fact, many large farming empires use very unsafe practices and the chemical runoff from their plants has even ended up contaminating nearby lakes and rivers. Avoid poisoning your garden and the world around you by staying organic.

Not Preparing for winter

Raised garden beds need to be protected for the winter. Many gardeners ignore this step, both with their raised beds or with flower beds directly in the ground. Then, come the next spring, they wonder why their soil is such low quality. This shouldn't be a surprise but it seems many beginners don't realize that they need to prepare for the winter the same way that the birds and bears do. The soil needs to be kept safe from the elements.

The easiest way to do this is to get a tarp from your local gardening center and use this over top of the raised beds. However, a more natural and rewarding way to do this is to spread a layer of compost over your soil and then a layer of mulching. This will keep your soil safe from the elements, while also letting the compost decompose and turn into nutrients to enrich the soil. Make sure that you get some protection down before the first major snow storm of the season.

Conclusion

A well-planned garden alongside the selection of the right soil is the secret to successful raised bed gardening. These gardening tactics are not new inventions; in fact, they have been practiced in some form or the other from ages. Raised bed gardens are becoming increasingly popular in the US today. Certain technical aspects of the planning may vary from region to region, but the fundamentals are the same virtually everywhere. If applied skillfully, these techniques can result in a far better production rate (as much as 4 to 10 times better according to some estimates) than what you would achieve through orthodox gardening methods in an average fertile land.

One of the most important factors that make raised beds so effective and efficient is that the crops get the chance to grow in just the right type of soil - deep, fertile and loose enough to yield higher production rate. This is possible because the overall condition throughout the setup is favorable towards proper soil drainage as well as aeration, which in turn enables plant-roots to penetrate deeper.

Apart from that, maintenance is also pretty easy in any raised bed garden. Removing weeds and rubbles hardly takes any time, enabling you to focus more on other important tasks such as watering the plants. Since the gardener will always be standing in the pathway, the plants never have to face the risk of being stepped on. Unlike the traditional gardening tactics, you can concentrate your soil amendment and improvisation efforts on the beds only, not on the pathway. This, needless to say, helps you save on both resources and time.

The appeal of raised bed gardening is that it hardly requires any special care or attention. The only factors that you will ever have to worry about are: watering the plants, planting and harvesting them at the proper time and periodically removing minimal amounts of weed from the garden. Whenever you harvest a plant, add some compost into the empty space and then replant.

The type of the soil as well as the wall material used for constructing the raised beds play a pivotal role in the overall health of the plants and your garden. Proper spacing between the plants is also crucial - if congested, they won't get enough room to grow freely. On the other hand, if there's just too much space in between them, your production rate will suffer and weeds are encouraged to grow. You also have to be careful to choose plants that will grow favorably in your climate.

The next step for you is to take a walk around your potential raised bed garden area and do some planning. Remember, if you have good sun, good soil, and plenty of water you're going to be okay. Good luck and happy harvesting!

Raising the bed by as much as 8 inches above ground level likewise makes sure much better drain. When utilizing raised bed packages there you will not need to enter the raised bed when doing garden upkeep along with having the ability to grow more vegetables due to the root space that is now offered to the plants.

You will require to water the raised bed typically enough that the plants are growing and the soil is damp without any standing water in any area in between rows. You must nevertheless prevent watering your plants with a hose pipe as this can make the plants end up being too damp which can draw in fungi along with other illness.

You can avoid illness from ruining your plants by including extra defense to the leading as well as bottom of your raised bed. And do not forget to put a weed barrier in between the ground and the soil for the raised planting bed.

For anybody that wishes to garden utilizing a tiered raised bed there is requirement to do some preparation well ahead of time. It likewise assists if you will put in the time to find out appropriate positioning for the raised flower garden bed to develop an excellent style in addition to choice up great light before doing anything else. You may wish to develop a sketch of your garden and put in locations reserved for the outdoor patio along with demarcate where you plan putting pathways.

Mulching the raised bed can likewise assist keep weeds at bay and making use of natural mulches is the very best method to go. In case your plants end up being impacted by soil borne illness you will require to alter the soil and after that continue with your gardening. This is much easier in a raised bed set as the soil is included in one location.

We talked about how we raised beds gardening and can show to be helpful for you, it is required to initially comprehend the benefits of the raised bed. In this regard it is rather apparent that such beds are extremely flexible and likewise quickly utilized and provide a variety of advantages that the traditional garden bed cannot use. A raised garden bed permits you to keep close control over how you blend soil so you can grow plants with soils that fit their development to get the finest outcomes.